Meditation and Reinventing Yourself

In lovingkindness)

[signature]

Meditation and Reinventing Yourself

Alex Mill

Zen Life Books

Meditation and Reinventing Yourself

Written, illustrated, and designed by Alex Mill
This book was originally created for Steve Chandler's
Reinventing Yourself Weekend, April 10-12, 2015
www.stevechandler.com

Alex Mill
Zen Life Coaching
Louisville, CO 80027

Website: www.zenlife.coach
Email: alex@zenlife.coach

ISBN-13: 978-1-7342391-1-9
ISBN-10: 1-7342391-1-5

Second Edition

For Steve

CONTENTS

FOREWORD:
WHY AM I UNHAPPY?

Once I wrote a book called *Reinventing Yourself* and it became a bestseller and helped me bring its teachings to many organizations and individuals during my career as a coach and teacher. That was decades ago, and although the book still sells well and seems to help people, it is not complete.

It was a reflection of what I'd learned up to that time, but it was missing a vital piece...a piece I've tried to put forth in my more recent books, but never have I done it so simply and clearly as Alex Mill does in this wonderful book right here, *Meditation and Reinventing Yourself*.

There was a hint of that missing piece right up in the front of the original edition of my incomplete book...a quotation from Wei Wu Wei:

> *"Why are you unhappy?*
> *Because 99.9 percent of everything you think,*
> *and of everything you do, is for yourself*
> *—and there isn't one."*

My book opened with that quote, but it didn't give the reader any clue about what it meant. Or what to do with it. It was intriguing, though, right? And on some level I must have intuited what it meant, and the freedom it pointed to, but I couldn't put that freedom into words.

Alex Mill has put it into words, and I am happy to say, he has also put it into pictures. His gifts as a cartoonist and illustrator are put to great use throughout this book, making his points all the more delightful and insightful.

Most "spiritual books" we read by great masters, teachers and sages are very wise, but also deep and heavy. The ones I buy and read are so rich and heavy with wisdom that it sometimes feels like it would take a forklift to get one of them from the lower shelf in the bookcase to my desk.

This book goes the other way.

There is a lightness to it that keeps you turning pages. That's not to imply that it's shallow. It is light-hearted in the sense that there is a light coming from the heart of it. And unlike so many spiritual books that say, "There is nothing to do! You have to just sort of hope this awakening happens to you!" Alex gives us plenty to do! Just follow his simple directions on meditation and fill in the easy blanks set up for self-inquiry as you read.

Even though he draws on the ancient traditions and sacred teachings of Zen Buddhism that he was steeped in for 14 years in the monastery, the presentation here is present-day practical. There are easy exercises to do and short blanks to fill out so that we can engage and experiment with what we are learning all along the way.

Why are we unhappy? It's a simple misunderstanding that this book clears up. All those self-critical thoughts and voices we encounter throughout our lives are unmasked here, in humorous and helpful ways, and shown to be figments of our imagination, and not to be taken seriously anymore. Breathe easy (literally) because they are not who we are.

What Alex and this book's teaching on meditation show us how to do is to nurture and cultivate the inner power and peace that have been our true identity all along. So, instead of reinventing yourself to be a better, stronger ego, you can drop all that and guide your attention to the breath and therefore inspiration itself...that same life-giving breath that leaves the contracted ego behind and reveals our intimate connection with all living things, all worlds, all universes and divine, infinite love.

Meditation has become very popular in western culture recently due to the positive results so many companies and individuals are receiving from its practice. The neuroscience studies on how it actually changes the brain are now plentiful and no longer in question.

Alex's work as a seminar leader and life coach verifies this daily. And his long years of focused devotion in the monastery give added power and respect to his work. He's not just now surfing a wave of popularity here, he's reaching way back and sharing his life.

The fact that he has done it in such a user-friendly and charming way, so easy for people like you and me to read and enjoy, is a gift. I plan to give this book to a lot of my clients, friends and family members, and I bet you'll do the same.

Steve Chandler
Birmingham, Michigan
January, 2020

PREFACE

I have written this book to read like an illuminated poetry book. Or a song. Or a mantra that repeats a consistent refrain throughout.

I filled it with personal stories, lessons, tools, exercises, metaphors, and teachings—ones that have impacted my life.

There is a bit of repetition.

I needed the lyrics and refrains to deepen my understanding and so I imagine they might help you do the same.

And just when the rhythm gets going, there are cartoons interspersed here and there to transmit the message on a whole new level. Perhaps humor will open up to insights!

The basic message in meditation is this:

Learn to direct your attention and all will be well. Stay open to guidance from Life. Develop a kind, loving relationship with yourself. Let compassion replace whatever relationship you may have with the voices in your head.

Pay attention to everything. Nothing is insignificant.

The basic encouragement is this:

Stay open. Resist the temptation to think you know. Make no conclusions or accept what I say as "the truth." Above all, embrace the spirit of repetition.

The heart accepts repetition because that is what the heart does. It is the beating wisdom of the universe.

Only the voices complain about repetition (ironically, ignoring their own repetitive complaints—the ones that cause us to suffer. Competing interests, I suppose...Methinks the voices protest too much!)

I leave you with Zen Master Shunryu Suzuki's suggestion:

"If you lose the spirit of repetition, your practice will become quite difficult."

Here's to a joyful practice filled with lots of intentional repetition!

INTRODUCTION:
MY PERSONAL MEDITATION STORY

I just wanted to say a little about myself to provide you some background for this book. In 1999, I stumbled upon Zen Buddhism by innocently wandering into a quaint new age bookstore with my girlfriend. I had absolutely no interest in anything remotely spiritual and I was going in there to tag along with her. I picked up a book off one table and began to thumb through it. The first few pages in and I was hooked. The author was talking about my life as though she was standing inside my head!

I had everything I thought should make me happy—and I wasn't. It's not that I was miserable, but I felt like there was something missing. A dissatisfaction and a sense that there must be more to life than just getting together with someone, earning money, and spending it on stuff. Soon after, I bought a Zafu (meditation cushion) and began meditating daily. Things started to change for me—life was slowing down and I discovered how I was put together. I was becoming kinder and more patient. People noticed that I was different.

After selling most of my belongings, my girlfriend and I traveled cross-country in the Zen monastery's direction. What started as a simple drop in turned into a request to see if I could stay for a month, which was granted to me. It didn't take long until I realized that I had found my new home.

I had just turned 30 years old, and I was living as a Zen Buddhist monk in a monastery on the path to ending suffering.

At the end of the summer in 2013, I left the monastery for several reasons, but my love for the practice and all that I had learned there stayed with me. I knew that I wanted to continue offering my experiences to keep the practice alive within myself. My teacher had told us, "You will do for the love of others what you would not be willing to do for yourself." If it required me to continue showing up for others with love and service, it would transform me with love. That was true in the monastery and it is true today.

I jumped right in and created a website, wrote and illustrated a small children's-style book, developed (and still offer) a month-long online retreat, and began coaching people one-on-one using the skills I had learned while living at the Zen monastery. Which I absolutely *love!!!* It reminds me so much of the facilitation I did while living as a monk.

My goal today is to assist as many people as possible through practice—to show them that there's a way to access happiness right here and right now. That it's not at the end of the rainbow. It's right here under their noses.

And it's a joy-filled process!

In lovingkindness,

Alex

MEDITATION IS A PRACTICE

I f you want to influence the quality of your life, you will want to make time for meditation.

And it doesn't take much. In the workshops I teach, I encourage participants to meditate every day for just five minutes. Not four and not six. Five.

That seems like a reasonable investment of time to make coming from such a bold statement like, "If you want to influence the quality of your life, you will want to make time for meditation."

But resistance people run into with just this short, simple addition to their day would surprise you.

Clients I've coached report endless distractions and challenges that arise as they take on meditation. One businessman told me he sat himself down on a meditation cushion, started his timer for five minutes, and was immediately bombarded by the voices in his head screaming bloody murder, arguing about all the time he was wasting. He was shocked at the uproar to *just five minutes!*

Which is why I encourage *just five minutes!* Because anything more than that could somehow appear like a big investment of time. It's hard to imagine that five minutes is impossible.

Everyone's got five minutes, right?

So start with five and then gradually add more time consciously when you cannot stand not doing more. But *only* after you have been successful meditating every day. You want to be successful. Otherwise, meditation can become this Herculean task that you might accomplish on most days. But the real power comes when you consistently practice it every day.

Set yourself up for success. It's a practice and you need to be kind, compassionate, and patient with yourself. Regularly doing less for success is the key.

HOW WILL MEDITATION MAKE MY LIFE BETTER?

I don't know.

I will share with you how meditation has transformed my life.

It has created the foundation upon which I can build every change I have ever wanted to make. It has trained me to direct my attention to what I want my attention to go to, which is the ultimate super power.

Imagine, under any circumstance—whether it be ideal or not—to be able to sit back and allow information to arise and fall away with complete relaxation and alertness. Instead of being plagued by thinking, I can be open to Life's guidance and wisdom to drop through into the clearing meditation has created on the cushion.

Perception of time slows down and urgency becomes a thing of the past. Inhibitions and resistance fall away. My creativity and every quality and characteristic about me increases exponentially. I can become truly myself—in fact, ten times myself!

Picture a clean conduit for Life to rush through you—all the blockages have been cleared. It's like Liquid Plumr® for the soul.

Everything I need to know is in direct contact with my consciousness and flows to me without impediment.

Instead of rehashing what I coulda/woulda/shoulda done, I'm available for insights and wisdom in *this moment* to inform and guide a future I want to create with what I have.

Worry, fear, and dread don't help.

Imagine someone who absolutely *needs* to be in the moment. For safety's sake. Say someone like a surfer who is out there in the ocean hanging ten.

Picture this surfer riding a huge wave.

Can you see how thoughts don't help the surfer?

What's the surfer doing? Paying attention to the wave!

Information about what to do comes via insights arising in the moment. There are no predetermined, premeditated actions or thoughts that can help.

What happens if the surfer on that massive wave focuses on what coulda/woulda/shoulda been done or worries about what will happen later in the day?

That's right. Wipeout!

And that's us, right? Wiping out all the time! Yet we were trained to go back into that wipeout machine (a.k.a. conditioned mind) to solve what we need to do about wipeouts. No amount of mental work will get us out of this trap alive! To paraphrase Einstein, we are blessedly called upon to solve this problem with a different mind than the one that created it.

Thinking and problem solving become just more distractions that pull us away from the present and into wipeouts.

So how do we cultivate this skill?

Enter meditation…

How to Meditate!

WOW! **COOL**

Tack this up in the place you will sit! 📌
(tacks not included)

WHAT YOU'LL NEED

* A place to sit in silence everyday.
* Something to sit on: a meditation cushion, chair, rolled up blanket, etc.
* A timer set to a time between 5 to 30 minutes.

HOW TO SIT!

Crown of the HEAD pushing up—which tucks the chin slightly

EYES OPEN & CAST DOWN at a 45° ANGLE (soft focus)

Spine straight & shoulders relaxed

JUST ♡ BREATHIN'

Hands in the COSMIC MUDRA (Mōō-drə)

sitting on the 1st third of the cushion

Facing a Blank wall

one leg in front of the other with KNEES on the floor

Variations:
You can kneel on the cushion

OR sit on a meditation bench

OR sit on the end of a stool or chair ANYWHERE!

Okay, I'm sitting. Now what?!!

① **BREATHE**: Inhale, Exhale, repeat. Take a breath in, and on the exhalation silently count "1." On the next, count "2." And so on up to "10." Then start again at "1."

② **PAY ATTENTION**: Your attention will begin to wander to your body, emotions, thoughts, and voices. Whenever you notice this—gently bring it back to the BREATH.

③ **SIT STILL**: Nothing to do. Nowhere to get. Just breathing!

④ **STICK WITH IT**: All sorts of stuff will come up. That's okay. We're just sitting with all of it. Every sit you do is a "good one." Resistance will arise. STICK WITH IT. Your HEART is STRONGER. BE KIND.

Keep your commitments!

©Alex Mill

HOW MEDITATION WORKS

I want to be clear with you I don't know everything about all the different styles of meditations out there. I am not an expert on meditation, nor am I even a guru, a master, or anything else.

I have only ever practiced the one meditation that I learned how to do before I went into the monastery where I trained for 14 years. It's the one I taught while I was there, and it's the one I continue to teach now that I'm out in the world.

So that's what I'm calling "meditation."

It has its origins in Zen Buddhism and is typically lumped in with mindfulness-based meditation practices.

Here's how it works.

Your attention can only be in one place at one time. In one of two places—either *here* or *not here*.

When you are not here, you are lost.

Ever notice that you are constantly distracted? Whether it be by others, things, situations, your mind, or social media?

When your attention is pulled away from where you want it to be, what is your experience? Loss of control? Overwhelm? Depression? Trauma? Lack of fulfillment? Procrastination? What else?

_____

_____

_____

_____

Have you also noticed how your attention rarely wanders toward thoughts about how happy you are, what you are grateful for, what you love, and the feelings of compassion? Not unless it's a setup for having the rug pulled out from under you to feel bad.

So let's just say that on autopilot, your attention is being directed for you. It's a big game of "look here" and "look there" and you just follow along with it.

That's everyday life for most folks—attention going all over the place like an untrained puppy getting into trouble.

Meditation is the arena in which you get to take back all of this lovely attention for yourself. Because you have this one precious life to live and you don't want to waste it for even a moment. Right?

Meditation is the training ground for you to learn this skill.

And the skill is, volitionally *directing your attention*.

The entire meditation posture is set up to support this. It allows you to be relaxed, yet alert. It is very specific. Every aspect was designed to maximize the benefits. Even sitting in front of a blank wall in silence, not moving, with your hands in the Cosmic Mudra and keeping your eyes open are intentional.

The rules are simple: Stay still and focus your attention on your breath.

There.

That's it.

No "clear your mind," "focus on the positive," "float off to Nirvana." Just sit and focus on your breath.

If your attention wanders from the breath (as it will) just redirect your attention back to the breath. Mindfully, compassionately, and diligently. That's what you are practicing. That's the muscle you are strengthening. This is your choosing muscle growing!

This simple practice, if done daily for five minutes (not four and not six), will transform your life.

Like any practice you do, the more you do it, the better you'll get. If you don't practice it, you won't get better. If you do it, you'll get better.

It's just like everything else in the world. Such as learning a new language, playing an instrument, and mastering a sport. It's the law of the universe.

No "good person" if you do it. No "bad person" if you don't.

Therefore, every meditation you do is good.

The only "bad meditation" is the one you don't do.

RESISTANCE TO MEDITATION

H ere's the fun part (or, in the beginning, the frustrating part.)
If you've ever tried to meditate before, you may have noticed that you:

Start strong, but eventually peter out. "I think I can, I think I can..."

Start wobbly, get consistent, and somehow, mysteriously forget to do it again. "Where'd it go?"

Start discouraged and overwhelmed, which leads to giving up right out of the gate. "Nope. Don't wanna!"

Start gung-ho with such high standards that it is just impossible to meet them. "Definitely not cut out for this!"

Start okay, do it for a while, but then the routine is threatened, you fall off the wagon, and you skip a day or two, which leads to a hard time bringing it back in again. "Dangit!"

Start doing it, things get better in your life, and then you quit because you are "fixed," only to find yourself back in the same suffering place you started. *"Aarrgh!"*

Start because of a daily program that ends when the program ends. "Hi and goodbye!"

Or some variation of the above. And you may have noticed that you do other things in your life like this besides meditation. Maybe this is how you do relationships? Or how you take on a hobby? Or engage in work situations?

This is because the sabotage system inside of us is the same and it sabotages all things in exactly the same manner. But more about that later...

THE VOICES IN MY HEAD
DO NOT LIKE ME

H ave you noticed the voices in your head?

When you catch on to the voices as less than friendly pests between your ears—things will change.

Because the biggest challenge to stay mindful, happy, peaceful, kind, and present is "the voice" of self-hate.

This isn't some psychological disorder I'm talking about. This is the constant stream of chatter that plays on-and-on like a bad radio station. It is mean to you; it is mean to others; it lies to you; it misguides you; it talks you out of what's good for you, and it talks you into what's not so good for you.

While I was at the monastery where I trained, I started a cartoon series attempting to depict how it worked. Humorously, I illustrated what we were all up against and what to do about it. The series started as "The Voices" cartoons (to reveal how suffering happens) and eventually ended up as "Voicebusters, Inc." (to show how to stop that.)

The biggest smokescreen the voices use to create suffering in our lives is to make us believe that it is "just *me*."

"It's just me thinking."

I hear this confusion in the language people use through phrases such as, "I beat myself up."

No, in fact, you don't. You don't beat yourself up. Why would you do that? You don't wake up in the morning and say to yourself, "Gosh, I wonder how much of a hard time I can give to myself today."

If you look closely—you'll notice that you *get* beaten up.

Have you heard any of the following?

You *loser!*

You *should have known better!*

You*'ll never get it right!*

You're so stupid!

When will you *ever learn?!*

Fill in the blank _____

Notice all the "Yous!" When something says *you* to you, it's talking *to* you. It's *not* you if it's talking *to* you. Right? What I hope you can see is that you are not the author of these accusations! You are the recipient. Getting present to the voices—what they say, when they say it, where they say it, and how they say it—will transform your relationship to life. You will catch on to their shenanigans and because of knowing how they work so intimately, you will see them for the unhelpful parasites they are.

We aren't attempting to deny their existence or push them away. This is because it's a waste of time and it doesn't work in the long run. Ignoring them only gives them more power to pounce on us when we least suspect them.

Instead, we are noticing them and learning everything we can about them—like masterful opponents on the playing field. We are hunting them down! We are using consciousness to see them for what they truly are. We are becoming the experts on them. As a result, they will lose their power. We will stop believing them.

The following exercise will help you start this process:

Write what the voices say to you.

Then highlight the phrase that is most believable to you, the one that gets you stuck and upset, derailed, and off-course. I'll start the ball rolling with one that shows up for me!

"You're so tired. You don't feel like working on that now. Tomorrow. Work on it tomorrow when you'll be fresh and ready to do it!"

Your turn:

_____

_____

_____

_____

_____

_____

Take nothing the voices say to you personally. They will try to make you feel bad about anything they can (even that you have voices in your head!) Your best strategy will be to go after them instead of waiting for them to come after you! Remember, you are the hunter now.

Expect them not to be pleased.

DOOR-TO-DOOR

In Zen Buddhist meditation, we silently count our breath on the exhalations. Take a breath in, then silently count "one" at the bottom of the exhalation. Take another breath in, then silently count "two" at the bottom of the next exhalation. And so on, until ten. Repeat at one. Easy peasy, right? Just direct your attention over-and-over again to the breath.

Ah, but distractions show up, right? Voices come around to pull your attention off the breath and onto them—onto the drama. They dash in like some roaming door-to-door salesperson who is trying to get you to open up and buy a little distraction. And it doesn't matter what it takes—whatever will get you to open your door! A random shopping list, a fantasy, a dread, or perhaps a mistake you made a long, long time ago.

All designed to lead toward suffering by endlessly rehashing them.

But you can drop that and come back to the breath *anytime*! It's your choice. It's what you are committing to by embracing a meditation practice. To direct your attention to the breath and to be present.

Until the next knock on your door gets your attention…

Exercise:

Write three places *your* attention habitually gets pulled away to:

1. _____

2. _____

3. _____

See if you can compassionately accept yourself no matter what you discover.

That's what we're practicing.

THE SECRET TO STAYING GROUNDED

P lain and simple.

Don't leave the ground.

Don't indulge the thinking. Don't noodle the juicy story.

Because nothing is more important than presence.

Your heart does not resist your body coming to silence and allowing your mind to inhabit the body.

Only the voices of resistance want you to leave the peace that is *who you truly are* to go visit the mind's Crazy Fun House of distorted mirrors and shifting floors. Why? So you can franticly search for peace. The peace that was who you were before you left. The peace that is you.

Stay at center and allow everything to come to you. Never leave center to indulge a problem, a concern, or a worry. Center is where your power is and it has the ability to transform everything.

Chasing after the world brings chaos.

Allowing it all to come to me brings peace.

—Zen Gatha

THE ART OF BEING HAPPY

T he art of being happy is really simple:

Stop engaging with the story in your head.

"Yeah but when I was a child, I..."

Nope.

Stop engaging with the story in your head.

And if you notice a story about the story in your head beginning to start, stop engaging with that too.

This is true compassion.

It takes care of everything.

Meditation is a beautiful metaphor for this practice.

Over-and-over again your attention leaves your breath.

Over-and-over again you bring your attention *back* to the breath.

That's all that's going on.

You are practicing pulling your attention away from suffering and redirecting it to the present where suffering does not exist.

But don't take my word for it. Have an experience of it for yourself.

Do it today.

Notice when you're lost in a story.

Drop it and bring your attention back.

Focus on your breath.

Repeat as needed.

ON THE RUNAWAY TRAIN OF WANTING

I could sum my life up before the monastery with this process:

Become excited by something.

Pursue that something.

Purchase or get that something.

Become obsessed with getting more-and-more of that something.

And then I would just keep looping around and around doing that process *all the time.*

So, here is an illustration of how this played out:

I was an artist who loved to create. I had a job that paid extremely well so I only had to work part time to afford the beautiful apartment I lived in, pay the bills, purchase the food, and buy the stuff I collected constantly. I told people that I was working part time so I could spend my free time on my artwork—"my passion in life."

Here's the funny (or rather, the frustrating) part. Whenever I would face some free time—time I specifically created so I could focus on my artwork—I felt *compelled* to avoid doing it. Sometimes I would get as far as putting up a blank piece of paper on the drawing board and stare at it. Then I would leave the apartment to go record shopping. Or book shopping. Or art supply shopping. Or record-book-art supply shopping. I would spend most of the day doing this.

Then I'd come home, put on one of the new CDs I'd bought, begin listening to it and then…

IT would happen…

"Wow! I need *more* of this stuff! This is *great!* What other music out there is like this?" And then I'd be off to the races again, looking that information up, calling around to see who had it. The music was playing in the background and I didn't care. I was out on the streets hunting down more of it.

This was *non-stop*.

I even started to do it with the meditation books I had discovered. I began collecting all of them, which is how I realized what was going on! The meditation books taught me about the process of dissatisfaction. And here I was *live* in 3-D doing that process while realizing it! I sat there dumbstruck with this insight. I saw the addiction. "Oh, my God! This is how I have been doing my *whole life*!"

I literally saw my whole life flash before me: I couldn't finish my meal without thinking of the dessert I would eat afterwards. I couldn't enjoy my book because I'd obsess about the video I would watch with my friends tomorrow. I was talking to a good friend, and all I wanted to do was go shopping for music.

This phrase from one of the meditation books stuck out in my mind:

One process does not lead to another. You can't "want" in order to "have." "Wanting" leads to more "wanting." "Having" leads to more "having." If you want to "have" just "have."

Of course! Of course! Of course!

I was caught on the runaway train of "wanting" in pursuit of "having." It would never give me what longed for because I was never present. I was always on to the next thing, never in the moment, and so joy was evading me.

I began to cry when I realized that I was on the wrong train going in the wrong direction!

Once I began meditating, I could articulate how I felt. I described my life as being stuck in an invisible box with myself while Life was happening "out there" around me. I was always out of touch with it. It was always beyond my reach. Nothing was meaningful, conversations were shallow, I was hiding behind my mask of interests, and I wasn't enjoying anything I thought I should.

What's worse, I saw everyone else caught up in doing the same thing. We were all screwed up and pretending like everything was just fine.

When I saw how it all worked, I realized that I didn't want to play this game anymore.

People can try to convince you to pursue your passions, to get what you want—that leading an extraordinary life is in doing something satisfying. But I learned that this isn't the way it worked.

I realized that I needed to learn firsthand how to become satisfied to lead an extraordinary life.

I needed to start, end, and be with satisfaction if I was to experience satisfaction.

LIVING A MINDFUL KINDFUL LIFE

From my personal observations, happiness does not seem to exist in the activities and things of this world. A person can dwell in paradise and be miserable while another person can live in squalor and be happy.

Happiness lives in our perspective of things and situations.

Happiness is a byproduct of where our attention goes.

I have also noticed that there can be no internal shift to happiness without first changing how we behave. We can't go on doing the same stuff that isn't working and expect different results.

Therefore, service was such an enormous component of my life when I was a monk. St. Francis put it perfectly when he said to "Preach the Gospel at all times. Use words if necessary."

Compassionate action is the key to change my view of the world.

I had experience-after-experience of joyfully showing up whole-heartedly in life as the antidote to any challenge. While I was at the monastery, I was the cook for many, many years. I could either show up and work day-in and day-out joyfully, or I could show up day-in and day-out miserably. The choice was entirely mine! I was showing up whether or not I was happy!

So that's when it occurred to me to see my day as an imaginary pie divided up into slivers of moments. I knew that I couldn't always choose what would fill those moments, but I could choose how I wanted to *be* in those moments. And when I *could* choose how to fill those moments, I would fill them with what supported me.

For example, today, when I wake up, I immediately sit and meditate. That's sliver one. Then I perform a simple ritual that involves yoga and a little chanting. That's sliver two. And then so on throughout my day.

Now doing the dishes shows up as one of those slivers too. I don't always want to do them, but I am going to. So this is when I ask myself, "How do I want to *be* while I'm doing the dishes?" Then I practice that.

And so on with the remaining slivers.

What slivers do you struggle with the most? How would you like to *be* that would change how you experience those slivers?

_____

_____

_____

WATCH OUT FOR THIS ONE!

My alarm went off this morning at 6:00 am to get me ready for a coaching call I had with a client at 7:00 am. I got out from under the covers and went to grab my morning liter of water with lemon. After drinking it, I immediately sat down to meditate.

This is my go-to practice since my monastery days—to meditate upon waking. I have found it to be immensely grounding. There's something about the act of formally sitting and directing my attention to the breath as soon as my eyes open that has been powerful. It seems to be the time when I am most susceptible to being "downloaded" with unhelpful fears, thoughts, voices, and concerns.

On a typical day, I would have continued on by doing my gentle yoga prostrations ritual for an extra half hour, but I prepared for the upcoming call instead.

And it was a rather powerful session. One in which my client had a breakthrough within the first forty-five minutes of our call. So we both agreed that she was complete and bowed out of the session rather than continue on for the remaining time.

I watched myself immediately go to some busy work after the call—the usual routine of checking emails and replying to them, re-viewing my to-do list, looking at my calendar, etc.

Then it occurred to me that I could do the rest of my morning practice.

"There's not enough time for that," came in the whispering voice.

I internally accepted this as true because I had another client to talk to that morning. Turning back to my busy work, my forehead scrunched up, and I asked myself, "Is that *really* true?"

As I sat there and did the math, I realized I had *two hours* before my next call! That was *way* more than enough time to do the prostra-tions *and* have breakfast! In fact, I had planned to do the rest of my routine after the first call.

I stood there, ready to begin my ritual, when the next line came in, "But you don't feel like it. You did plenty of yoga last night. Take it easy on yourself…"

I had to smile because of the pause it gave me.

It was so believable! And I was soooo incredibly close to accepting it as a valid reason to ditch the routine.

Without turning back to my computer, I finally said—

"No, you will not win today! I've been down this road with you before. I have a commitment and I intend to keep it. I always feel better when I do what I say I will do. Besides, I enjoy my ritual! There's yoga, chanting, incense, and a declaration of my intentions. What's not to love?"

As I finished my blissful practice and moved on to breakfast, I felt immense gratitude for the practice that has given me back my life and made it possible for me to help others do the same.

How does the voice trick you into some shady stuff with its "helpful" advice? How does it pretend to "care" so much about you by guiding you off course and out of integrity?

How does the voice "assist" you? What are its dubious lines?

_____

_____

_____

Please remember that your insights are all that matter. You aren't paying attention so you may "fix" yourself, (because you are not broken.)

Take on an attitude of a super sleuth. Bring your life into curiosity and wonder.

You are a remarkable being worthy of your attention—treat yourself like one!

NO WAS NOT AN OPTION

O ne of the biggest gifts I received from living at the monastery was the gift of no escape. Or I should say, the gift of dispelling the illusion that I could escape from myself.

In the world, I could get away with avoiding whatever threatened me. I could surround myself with what made me feel comfortable, safe, and secure. In this way, I never had to change or grow a lot, and not in any significant way. I could always take a detour to what I liked and what I wanted.

In fact, in the world, setting up my life this way is ideal. Getting what you want is right. Right? Everybody else is doing it.

Conversely, the monastery didn't take what I wanted into consideration *at all*. It loved me too much to let me settle for this.

At the monastery, the only response to any task was "yes" or "goodbye."

In the beginning, they gave me tasks such as cleaning outhouses, prepping vegetables in the kitchen, or weeding in the garden.

Then my work moved on to more complex tasks like handling power tools and driving the monastery vehicles.

Then they asked me to supervise other people doing those cleaning tasks and crew-related work.

Soon, threatening everything inside of me, they asked me to be responsible for an entire department—such as being the cook, or the gardener, or running the online business, (at one point, I was doing all three at once!)

To bring on the sleepless nights, I was next asked to do the terrifying task of facilitating groups and offering one-on-one guidance appointments with people. These were perhaps the most intense experiences of all. The voices screamed, "You don't know how to do this!"

But what could I say? No was not an option.

Because of paying attention and dropping the stories and focusing instead on the tasks at hand, I received the great gift of learning to love learning. I reinvented myself into a man who could be ready for *anything* and avoided *nothing*.

I cooked for retreats with over thirty participants; I assisted with our projects in Africa; I built buildings; I created a cartoon series that taught people how suffering occurred in human beings and how to end that. I did things that terrified me, excited me, and pushed my limits.

I rose through the resistance because I wasn't allowed to indulge the crappy voice in my head that believed I couldn't do that or that something was beyond me.

It's what I was learning since the first day I showed up at the monastery: Either go into the kitchen to chop carrots and be miserable or go into the kitchen to chop carrots and be happy. The choice was mine. I was going into the kitchen to chop carrots, regardless.

THE WISDOM OF NO ESCAPE

At the monastery where I trained, retreatants as well as new monks, were plunged into working meditation right away.

What I always loved was that no matter who you were or what your previous experience was, they always showed you exactly how to do whatever they asked you to do. Even if you were a "Master Chef," they showed you how to chop carrots the way we chop carrots.

I always felt immense love and compassion in this training process because what it eliminated right off the bat was unspoken expectations. No one had to wonder what the result should be. The monk or retreatant being trained knew *exactly* what was to be done.

Better ideas were also off the table. Even if the "Master Chef" knew a better way to cut those carrots and began sharing, the "Master Chef" was promptly ignored with a polite bow and the carrot chopping demonstration continued. The goal was to be present to the task at hand, settle into a beginner's mind, and watch as the urgency arose to BE someone useful, knowledgeable, or even *right*.

When all of us were asked to do these tasks, there was also an underlying message of "*nothing* is beyond you". No matter what your expertise or skill level, you were shown how to do it. So if cooking wasn't your thing, that's okay. It doesn't have to be. No one said you had to know how to do it or even like it. In fact, this was your golden opportunity to learn how to not only like it, but perhaps even to *love it.* Or to see clearly how you suffer because you don't like it.

Those were essentially our two choices: Do it and suffer or do it and be okay.

Everyone was adequate to her or his own experience.

If you didn't want to do the job—well, too bad. It's not about what you want, or what you prefer, or how you feel. There was no other job you will be given. This was the one. It's a snapshot of your life in miniature. Here's who you are in this moment. What's that like?

I had a love/hate relationship with this wisdom of no escape. Because I had no choice but to do what I was asked to do. I had to overcome many bouts of resistance. If I was asked to work in the kitchen, I worked in the kitchen. If I was asked to be the Cook, I became the Cook. If I was asked to be the leader of the retreat, I became the leader of the retreat. There was no saying "no."

In contrast to how life works outside the monastery, people can spend their whole lives avoiding what they don't want and gravitate toward what they want. In fact, that's popular and what's seen as "conventional wisdom." Just do what you love and avoid unpleasant things. Right? Doesn't everyone do that?

As a result, almost nobody ever learns or grows. There's no one out here to show us how to risk ourselves. The voice of resistance is our sole authority. It is loud and at the first sign of "I don't feel like it," we bail on ourselves.

There's also no one standing in our corner saying, "Come over here. It's awesome over here. There's nothing to be afraid of. I'll even hold your hand through it all."

But this is what we so desperately need.

We need someone to play this coaching role in our lives.

The exercise for today is to practice being that coaching presence for yourself. In a task that you normally approach with procrastination, avoidance, or dread—like taking out the trash, cleaning a mess, or plunging a toilet—see if you can practice simply doing it. Imagine having someone you love and who loves you there with you. What would that experience be like?

Imagine this person expressing words of encouragement, care, and understanding for you. Phrases like, "Yeah, I know you don't want to do this, but I'm right here with you and together we'll get this done." Or, "I wonder how you could make this fun?"

Be that loving presence you had always wanted for yourself. Your life will transform when your relationship with yourself transforms.

HOW I LOST EVERYTHING

"Someone once asked the Buddha skeptically, 'What have you gained through meditation?'

The Buddha replied, 'Nothing at all.'

'Then, Blessed One, what good is it?'

'Let me tell you what I lost through meditation: sickness, anger, depression, insecurity, the burden of old age, the fear of death. That is the good of meditation, which leads to nirvana.'"

—Excerpt from The Dhammapada

Until I lost everything, I spent a period of time at the Zen monastery depressed. After the initial high of entering the monastery and the thrill of learning new practices, tools, and skills had passed—I was left for months on end with a feeling like I was in my own *Groundhog Day*. I would wake up wishing I was out in the world so I could meet new people, talk to them, buy stuff, and lead a normal life. My daily struggle involved trying to find anything good or meaningful in the senseless tasks I was asked to repeatedly do.

"Alex, please work in the Kitchen today. In lovingkindness, Work Director." I could have saved them paper and effort if I'd re-posted that note back on the message board to myself for another five years.

Funny enough, when I had the opportunity to visit my family for a week once a year, I chose to stay in silence instead of doing what I had longed to do. At first, I'd drive out to the mall because I was dying to go there. I'd make it as far as standing in the middle of the Best Buy with all the latest gadgets surrounding me—and I would feel empty. What was the fascination with all this stuff? I saw the people roaming the aisles like automatons, miserable and addicted to this junk. So I'd walk out empty-handed and confused. The kicker was, no sooner was I back at the monastery when the same longing for stuff returned.

That's when I saw the irony of depression. I discovered that my attention was addicted to the story of how I was not getting what I wanted, how I was alone, and how there was nothing here for me.

The training I undertook was nothing short of mastering where my attention stayed. As long as it remained with me, there was no room for anything else. Like a dog with a bone, I kept my attention directed to end this cycle.

That's how I lost everything.

MY FAVORITE SPORT

While I was training as a monk, I opened up my bank account in a nearby city. Mostly I managed my account online, but one day I needed to complete a transaction in person. Along with the usual questions, the service specialist asked me my security question, "What is your favorite sport?" I promptly answered, "Meditation," at which point we both had a good laugh.

But it's true! It really was my favorite sport, and it is very much like a sport.

In the game of meditation, I am constantly training my attention to stop wandering. When it wanders, I "lose" (because as a result, I go unconscious and I eventually suffer). When it stays with me, I "win" (because I pay attention and experience presence, happiness, and clarity).

It's a heated match that always shifts from moment-to-moment. No snoozing or watching from the sidelines in this game! Luckily, it's all practice and I am always ahead for practicing.

As I've discovered, *practicing never made me worse at anything.*

Here's how life appears to work: My attention can be here in this moment *or* I can lose it in opinions, judgments, beliefs, fantasies, speculations, distractions, and just plain yuckiness.

One of two places: Here or not here.

Therefore: My life experience *depends* on the focus of my attention.

By habit, it wanders off into trouble.

I don't know how many of you go *unconscious* and as a result have your mind wander to what you are grateful for and how much you love and appreciate yourself, life, and the universe—but that's *not* where my mind typically wanders.

I can find my mind straying down the dark alleys of what's wrong and not enough, how there's more I should do, have, and be. Lost in the past or the future. Or obsessed with the current distraction my mind is impulse shopping with at the moment.

So mastering this wily attention appears to be where the gold is in this sport. And since happiness *exists* where my attention goes—it only makes sense to build my attention muscles to keep me playing in the present. Over-and-over-and-over again.

© Alex Mill

WHOSE IDEA WAS IT
TO DO YOGA AT 6 AM ANYWAY?

One thing I love observing with compassion is the process of self-hate. Some folks call it resistance, some call it procrastination—some call it the devil incarnate! I'm used to calling it self-hate, cause that's what it feels like to me, (although devil incarnate can get close sometimes.)

So here's the scenario: The night before, I get super-jazzed about doing yoga at 6:00 am, (anyone else out there who gets super-jazzed about exercising early in the morning the night before?) I go to bed and set the alarm so I can be sure I don't sleep through my commitment. I pull the covers over me in my warm flannel sheets and snuggle into my pillow with a smile on my face. The star-studded movie of Mighty Me doing rock-solid power yoga in the morning while the sun is on its way up flickers on the screen of my imagination.

It's gonna be good.

Fast forward to 6:00 am...with that alarm making an intense ruckus.

"That %#!!* alarm!"

My eyes roll in their sockets and I curse the idiot who thought getting up out of bed at 6:00 am was a good idea—let alone doing something as *ridiculous as yoga!*

I sigh and grumble.

After shutting the alarm off, I habitually roll over onto one side and dimly stare into space through crumbly peepers.

And then it happens. The Great Debate and The Bargaining for My Immortal Soul begins:

> *You don't really feel like getting up.*
>
> *You could do yoga later in the afternoon or tonight.*
>
> *Or even tomorrow...*
>
> *You just did yoga the other day.*
>
> *You really don't feel like it.*
>
> *How about yoga every other day?*
>
> *What are you trying to prove, anyway?*
>
> *What difference does it make if you do yoga now or later?*
>
> *It's too cold and dark to do yoga. Better to wait until it's warmer and brighter.*
>
> *Tomorrow, there's always tomorrow. That's why God created tomorrow.*

Maybe just a few more minutes in this warm, cozy, comfy bed and then see how you feel…

Eventually one of these hook-line-and-sinkers nabs me and drags me toward the desired outcome: Not doing yoga, and ultimately—feeling bad.

Here's how I lay out the process:

1. The Set-Up
2. The Follow Through
3. The Beating

The Set-Up happened the day before with the fantasy of how yoga would be. Expectation and the promise of perfection.

The Follow Through is the resistance that meets the commitment. If, however, I had committed to eating a box of donuts, drinking a gallon of coffee, or even playing video games first thing in the morning—I would have gotten nothing but "Hey, what a great idea! Party time!"

But no.

I decided to do something that would take care of me, make me feel good, and probably energize my entire day and set a good tone for everything to follow. This is the reason I call it self-hate. 'Cause the insidiousness of the whole process is that it leads to The Beating.

Let me rustle up the voices again for you. Here's what The Beating has to say:

Geez, you didn't do yoga again!

What a loser!

You can't do anything you've committed to!

And you wonder why your life is crappola?

Some discipline—and you think you *can* help *others?*

ha*!*

Physician heal thyself.

What a charlatan!

That's right, yet one more thing you can't get right.

After spending a sufficient amount of time being pounded into the earth—having traded the possibility of doing yoga and feeling good for a morning dose of "Feel Like Doo-Doo"—the following may creep in around mid-day:

You know, you can always do yoga tomorrow…

That's right! All is not lost!

This could be a good time to create that schedule you've al-ways wanted to follow.

Remember when you made that schedule, and you followed it for half-a-day?

Boy! That was a smokin' half-day!

Let's do that *again!*

And put yoga on at 6:00 am!

Heck, why not 5:00 am? You want to see the sunrise, don't you?

Score!!!

I hope you can see the cycle back to The Set-Up.

I'm being set up.

Again!

More expectations, more opportunities for failure, more feeling bad.

All of this dialog could turn in to an excuse for doing unfortunate behaviors. For instance, since the rainbow just showed up and tomorrow is looking brighter, I may just get talked into downing that box of donuts and that gallon of coffee.

Why not?

I deserve it! I'm the superhero again going to tackle yoga at 5:00 in the morning, aren't I? Heck, superheroes need reinforcements and treats and the "good stuff" in life. If I've been suckered into this drama, (read "yet another Set-Up") then what follows is no surprise: The Beating.

How could you eat every $%! donut in that box?*

You feel like excrement.

Have you no self-control at all?

Boy, you really need help.

Time to roll out the diet and regimen, again...

This process always amazes me. I admire the geniuses who concocted it because it truly deserves a patent. A real guarantee for misery.

Look to see what *your* version of this process is. Do you try to lose weight? Do you try to eat healthier foods? Do you try not to shop so much? Whatever it is, see how this shows up for you.

Write out what the voices say:

The Set-Up

_____

_____

_____

The Follow Through

_____

_____

_____

The Beating

_____

_____

_____

HELP! MY IDENTITY IS KILLING ME!

I once coached a woman who was incredibly stuck in her life. She worked two jobs to support her family, ran herself ragged by all of her self-imposed responsibilities, found herself obligated doing everything for everybody, had no time for herself, and contemplated "ending it all" as a viable way out of her life. In fact, she tried.

She claimed that no one around her took responsibility for anything—her husband did little to nothing, her kids spent the money she earned freely, and her own mother depended upon her for her care. Meanwhile, other sisters in her family could help take care of their mother (one even lived closer) but didn't.

Even when she was growing up, she had to work for everything she wanted while others *got* what they wanted.

After a bit of time talking to her about what was creating these situations, I saw there was a predominant personality inside her who was running the show.

The part of her that could not say "no." The part of her who wanted to be liked and approved. The "selfless one."

And because self-hate had a hold of it all, it pinned her into a no-win situation.

Saying "no" wasn't possible because the voices in her head racked her with guilt if she turned anyone away. Likewise, she resented anyone who imposed anything upon her and got her to say "yes" to something she couldn't say "no" to.

Guilt and resentment were the underlying addictions.

What we both got present to was the enormous damage this process was creating in her life.

I attempted to portray what I saw to her: No one needed to be a grown up as long as she was around—not her husband, not her kids, not her mother, not even her coworkers because *she* would do it *all*. In fact, having her do everything made their lives a luxury! They were happy with this arrangement and couldn't sympathize with her struggles—they didn't have to!

The analogy I used to describe to her how typical relationships work was through the use of this model: the roof of a house. So for simplicity, a roof is two slanted boards that press into each other to create the form. The boards each rely on the other to be a roof. If one of them tips and refuses to play its role, the whole thing collapses.

The same is true when relationships form.

Here's an example: A man comes over to me and "criticizes something I do." (This is in quotes because that's my interpretation.) I explain myself, but no matter how I attempt to defend my point, this man looks at me like I'm crazy. And then I say to myself, "Oh no! *the look!*" I feel bad even though I don't agree with him. I feel misunderstood, wrong, and alone. I doubt my perspective and wonder if anyone will ever understand. I wonder if I should just give up. Who I end up becoming is someone who doesn't share how I feel because I am tired of defending myself. I'm tired of being misunderstood.

All of this is an internal process going on inside of me. Nothing really happened except that some man came over and said something to me I heard as "criticism." He was one board, and I was the other. Together, we created "a roof"—my internal experience of what happened.

Other people presented with this situation could have responded in many different ways! For example, you could have heard what he said and replied, "Thanks for your opinion" and went along your business. Someone else could have shooed him away and told him to mind his own business. Another person could have engaged with him in a conversation unrelated to the topic and had a lovely chat.

The trap with identity is that it makes everything seem believably real! Because that is how we've *always* done it! Trigger ➤ thought ➤ emotion ➤ knee-jerk reaction.

Like an impersonal machine!

But when you change your role, you change the roof. The structure cannot exist without your participation. See for yourself.

Exercise:

With no need to change anything about yourself for now, see if you can spot at least one dominant personality in your life through

which you see the world. Notice how it shows up in your relationships, your career, your interests, and your life.

What are some things this part says to justify its viewpoints? What
kinds of statements or questions does this part say or ask?

Without judgment, what is the impact of believing these viewpoints? What is possible (and impossible) for you because of holding
onto this stance?

_____

_____

_____

_____

_____

_____

THE SIMULTANEOUS INTERPRETER!

"It ain't what you don't know that gets you into trouble. It's what you know for sure that just ain't so."
—*Mark Twain*

One monk at the monastery shared how the voices in her head translated the world she experienced into the meaning that she then carried around with her. She said it was like having her own "simultaneous interpreter."

That idea stuck with me and became the inspiration for this cartoon.

If you've ever been in situations where you've repeatedly drawn the same conclusions, chances are good you're buying into a story that The Simultaneous Interpreter is selling you. Take a step back and question the authority in your head. Get it that everything you experience is a *projection* coming from *you,* and the only thing you ever get to experience is *yourself.*

Exercise:

Take a situation from your own life in which you are assuming some kind of meaning.

Notice if the story is upbeat or challenging.

Write out what the voices in your head say about it.

See how they show up in other areas of your life.

Jot down any other insights you had from doing this exercise.

PERFECT IMPERFECTIONS

"There's no need to be perfect to inspire others. Let people get inspired by how you deal with your imperfections."
— Ziad K. Abdelnour

Really? Or are you perfect exactly as you are?!

Some may say, "I've always wrestled with that one... Define *perfect*? Because... if we *are* already perfect... what's the motivation for improving?"

How about *perfect=what is*?

Often perfect gets lumped in with *ideal* or *expectation,* which is Fantasy/Suffering-Land. Because, really, when will you *ever* be perfect under those standards? When have you ever? Is anyone ever thrilled with what they have because of those standards?

Self-improvement is a sham. There is no self to improve.

Try this for motivation:

You are the love of your life. Life is amazing with endless possibilities, and it's an incredible joy to take part in it 100%. You wake up every day to go all-out with everything because that is what you were put on this earth to do. Can you see the world from this perspective?

The Fire In The Song
by David Whyte

The mouth opens
   and fills the air
      with its vibrant shape
until the air
   and the mouth
      become one shape.
And the first word,
   your own word,
      spoken from that fire
surprises, burns,
   grieves you now
      because
you made that pact
   with a dark presence
      in your life.
He said, "If you only
   stop singing
      I'll make you safe."

And he repeated the line,
   knowing you would hear
      "I'll make you safe"
as the comforting
   sound of a door
      closed on the fear at last,
but his darkness crept
   under your tongue
      and became the dim
cave where
   you sheltered
      and you grew
in that small place
   too frightened to remember
      the songs of the world,
its impossible notes,
   and the sweet joy
      that flew out the door
of your wild mouth
   as you spoke.

Big question for you:

What audacious life would you create for yourself if those crappy voices didn't get between you and everything else?

Can you feel how they are holding you back? Do they say the following?

> *You're not ready yet.*
>
> *You still have soooo much more to learn and do before you can x, y, or z.*
>
> *Who do you think you are?*
>
> *You don't feel like it.*
>
> *You don't have the time, the money, the energy, the talent, the _____.*
>
> *Tomorrow. You can do it tomorrow!*

Life is waiting for you to ditch the voices, put on your polka dot jumpsuit, dance the funky chicken, and sing at the top of your lungs.

It's waiting patiently for you to wake up and choose something much, much bigger for yourself.

Will you stop being so stingy and selfish and *share* with us already?

HOW TO SIT STILL WITH EMOTIONS

You are a buoy in the ocean.

Imagine the waters around you.

Sometimes they are gentle. Lapping against you.

At other times they are gigantic waves, crashing over you. Over-and-over. Unrelenting and violent.

Because they are the waters in the ocean.

But you don't move.

Because you are the buoy.

And that's just what the buoy and the waters do.

THE EMOTIONAL ROLLER COASTER

Drama, highs-and-lows, and emotional turbulence seem to make the world go round. I see this on the daily news and I see it in my personal life. One day I appear to be "winning" in the game of life; on the next day, I'm "losing." Like the sports newscaster from the Seventies announced, it's "the thrill of victory and the agony of defeat."

And it doesn't take much. I feel a rush of adrenaline when lots of people like my Facebook post. And then the next minute a voice comes in to say, "Who cares? It means nothing. You're stupid for caring," and I crash into misery.

So today, I will share a very simple tool to map out your internal territory and take the mystery out of these random soap operas.

Before I do this, I will present a simple four-step model or framework upon which it rests. It's based upon a process called the "Battering Cycle," (now called "The Cycle of Abuse") developed by Lenore E. Walker to explain patterns of behavior in an abusive relationship.

Here's how it goes:

1. Stress builds from the pressures of daily life and the need to be "perfect.

2. In the traditional model, one partner beats the other to release the pressure. This is the coping behavior.

3. Both feel relieved. It would eventually happen. Thank goodness it's over now. But both feel bad; it's horrible that this just happened.

4. They resolve never to let this happen again. They strive to be "perfect."

But no matter what their resolve, nothing seems to change. They always end up at step one again and then cycle round-and-round.

There's the emotional low from the stress, the emotional high of the coping behavior, the emotional low from the results of the coping behavior, the emotional high from the decisions to be perfect, and then back to the emotional low from the stress from this.

This battering cycle plays out internally too.

Here are a few examples of how it happens:

Example 1:

1. *I have to create a big report for work and feel overwhelmed.*

2. *I avoid it by cleaning my room from top to bottom.*

3. *I feel good because I just spent that energy, and the room is clean. I feel bad because I avoided doing the report and I still have to do it!*

4. *I resolve to only do the important work first from now on. I "buck up" and just do it.*

Example 2:

1. *The night before, I plan to meditate first thing upon waking and I go to bed super excited about it.*

2. *In the morning, I fall prey to hitting the snooze button and sleep instead.*

3. *I feel good because I love spending time in bed. I feel bad because I never got to meditate. I'm upset because I never do what I commit to.*

4. *I resolve to try again tomorrow. This time, I'll do it!*

Example 3:

1. *I want to lose weight and so I join a gym.*

2. *I'm intimidated by the thought of working out. Not only that, but I've had a hard, stressful day and I just need to wind down so I stay home and watch television and eat junk instead.*

3. *I feel good because I avoided the fear and got some goodies to boot. I feel bad because I didn't lose the weight I said I wanted to and not only that but I probably gained more!*

4. *I resolve to force myself to go to the gym next chance I get.*

Do you see the pattern? Can you see how this process plays out in your own life?

Take a moment now to jot down what your version of this process looks like. Pay attention to how you do this.

Remember, awareness is *everything*. The first step to making different choices is to see *how* you make the ones you do now. Don't let "feeling bad" and the voice of abuse interfere with your exploration. Stick with it. Seeing is acceptance and acceptance leads to change.

What do *you* see?

Stress of being perfect

_____

Coping Behavior

_____

Feel good/feel bad

_____

Decision to be perfect

_____

ROUND-AND-ROUND-WE-GO

The next tool I would love to offer you is one I call "The Voices Chain." It's an illuminating game you can play that will help you see *how* the voices work in your life. No more wondering what they do behind the scenes. By following these simple steps, you can create a map through any situation that will reveal their process.

Note: This game is more involved than some others in this book. Get up, stretch, walk around a bit, and then settle in for at least a half-hour to explore.

What you will need to play:

- A large sheet of paper (or some wall space)
- Small, Post-It style notepaper (with a sticky side to adhere to the wall or large paper)
- Something to write with

Here's how to play:

Step one:

Identify an issue you would like to work with. Perhaps it's procrastination, or yelling at your partner, or not being able to say "no" to people, or whatever you see as a reoccurring pattern in your life. Then pick a real situation that happened recently.

Step two:

Determine a starting point. What kicked this off? For example, in the procrastination scenario, it could be:

"Got a terrible email from my boss that needs a response."

Step three:

Identify what the voice in your head says.

For example:

Oh !#@, an email from the boss!*

You're in trouble!

This is awful!

Jot these comments on the sticky notes—one comment per note—and then put them up on your wall or large sheet of paper.

Step four:

Ask yourself, "What happened next? What do I hear (from the voice) next?" Then continue to take dictation on the voices.

For example, (in this scenario):

You can answer the boss's email later once you've calmed down.

It wasn't your fault.

The boss will never believe you.

Write these down on the Post-It notes and add them to the wall or paper after the first set. Remember, this is what you hear in your head.

Step five:

Repeat step four. These stickies will make a "Voices Chain" that link what you hear in your head throughout the situation.

Pay attention to everything as you do this. Be open to insights. Don't let the voices use any of this to judge you. This game takes what goes on inside of your head to torture you and tosses it out in front of you so you can see it.

Awareness is freedom.

THE DUALITY BATTLE

Have you ever wanted to do something—and equally *not* wanted to do that very thing?

If you have ever caught yourself debating with yourself (over which box of cereal to purchase, whether to stay where you are or move someplace else, ditch the relationship you are in or hunker down for the long haul), you may have been embroiled in a *duality battle.*

This is common. In fact, it is the primary way that the voice keeps us in suffering and dissatisfaction.

But before I go on much further, why don't you have an experience of it for yourself?

Find a situation in your life where you see yourself in a duality battle—one in which you experience a strong pull in one direction and an equally strong pull in another. Make a list of voices you hear on one side and then make a list of voices you hear on the other. Write the language you hear in your head for all of it.

Here's an example.

The topic is: *Stay Where You Are or Go.*

Under the first heading, *"Stay,"* the voices say:

> *Your neighbors are awesome.*
>
> *Your rent is good, and it's close to work.*
>
> *This is home.*
>
> *The bills at the new place will be ridiculous.*
>
> *You hate unexpected surprises.*
>
> *You don't do well with change.*

The next heading is: *Move to a New Place.* Here, the voices say:

The new pad will be luxurious.

The new place will be near the cool shopping centers.

The gang will be impressed with this new place.

Face it, the overall neighborhood you live in now is going to waste.

You're tired of the same-old, same-old.

You need more excitement in your life.

Your turn:

Look over your lists. What do you notice? What does it feel like to have this going on in your head? Can you see a theme? Where else does this process play out in your life?

No judgments, please.

To consider: If there were no self-hating voices in your head that made either choice a problem, then you could pick *anything* and be okay with it. In fact, you could pick it and then decide a week later that you wanted something else entirely.

Picking either side is not a "problem."

Really!

What is the problem?

Regret, feeling bad, judgment, fear, lost opportunity, ruin, doom, failure, homelessness, death...

Basically, a story!

And it can be absurd with choosing a box of cereal, right? But there it is—just as fever pitched as if I was deciding between life and death itself!

I can laugh because I've been there! Head cast down, tortured in the aisles, reading labels and comparing prices, picturing my life with either, imagining how both taste, frustrated and ready to just walk away without either. Or toss both boxes across the store!

Now consider: What would you have liked in the situation you were stuck in? What would have helped?

Note: We're not attempting to draw conclusions from any of this. We are not trying to have "the good/right life" by picking "the correct thing." That's just part of the machine. That's feeding into the system!

We are also not using willpower to defeat the voices.

We are bringing awareness to the process the voices of resistance used to keep us stuck.

By catching them, we are gradually turning on the light in our darkened room. When the light gets turned up, we *see* the hole we fall into over-and-over again because we were walking in the dark. But in the light, we don't fall into it. There's no reason to. We *see* it for what it is. So we walk around the hole, hop over the hole, boogie on past the hole, or have no relationship to the hole at all.

That's what is possible. Can you *see* the difference?

COLOR OUTSIDE THE LINES

I 've always *been this way.*

I am...

I can't do that.

I never...

I should...

These phrases define what is possible and what is impossible for you. They create the boundaries in which they give you permission to move around. The more you believe them with your thoughts, the more you speak them with your words, and the more you act them through your deeds, the deeper the grooves become in your life and the more you become them.

In fact, these aren't the only phrases that create limitations. Any thoughts or stories that play out—"positive" or "negative"—put a box or a grid around undefined possibility.

In every moment, you are a blank canvas. An empty glass. A vast universe awaiting a mark! From that mark, you can place another. And then another.

Newness only arises from this "beginner's mind" openness, innocence, and wonder. Being present. With eyes wide open. Heart wide open and accepting.

It's the big *yes* to how it is. It's the big *and* to how it can be.

What will you create today? How will you "color outside the lines" of your life?

Look to see where those lines are. Finish these five phrases:

I've *always* been _____

I am _____

I can't _____

I never _____

I should _____

What do you tell yourself you are? What do you say is possible or impossible? What do you believe?

Write them all out.

_____

_____

_____

_____

Then, how would you go about challenging them? What would be on the other side of each limiting belief? And I'm not just talking about "the opposite." It could be something unexpected.

Be open to surprises.

Secret Tip: You aren't doing this to create "bigger and better" beliefs about yourself and Life—regardless of how much bigger and better they would feel compared to the "negative," limiting ones. "Positive" beliefs can be just as limiting.

Can you see why?

Question beliefs. What purpose do they serve? What effect do they have in your life?

Notes:

_____

_____

_____

_____

_____

_____

_____

_____

_____

THE LEAK!

Here's a little confession.

The following cartoon is an autobiography.

It represents an internal process that I have repeatedly fallen for—in *Voicesville*.

Perhaps some of you can relate to this communication trap. The harmless "Oh, I'll tell that to them later. It's not urgent *yet*. Wouldn't want to bother them now with this trivial thing..."

And I succumb to this resistance over-and-over again—until it becomes *super urgent* and things break down and I *really bother them* through my lack of communication. Now they are really upset.

This sets up the cycle in which I dread communication next time.

I had a breakthrough when I realized that it wasn't the communication that was received poorly. It was how I was set up *not to communicate,* or communicate incompletely, that made the untimely communication a disaster.

It would have been so much cleaner to have had said something at the very beginning when the insight to communicate occurred to me.

But that's the trap the voices get us with. They override life's love for us through their terrible advice, urgency, and fear.

They talk us into doing that which is harmful to us and talk us out of doing that which would take care of us.

Look into your own life to see if that's so for you.

One more thing I wanted to share with you. When I was a kid, I saw the Space Shuttle disaster with Christa McAuliffe (the school-teacher who would go to space). I remember it distinctly. My brother and I were off from school because of the weather, and I was watching it on the television in my room.

I remember the heartbreaking ball of fire as the shuttle exploded.

After the sadness of the tragedy began to fade, I remember the gnawing feeling inside of me. I projected what must have been going on for the person who approved the take off.

I didn't know it then, but I sensed that whoever it was had been overtaken by the voices just like the main character in my cartoon. Somehow, this person knew there would be a problem, but ignored it.

"The O-rings can't take this cold, but all of America is waiting for this to happen, and these delays are disappointing others…"

I created this cartoon to remind me I am embracing communication with compassion. It is compassionate to communicate timely and clearly.

NOTHING MEANS ANYTHING

A young woman I was coaching once asked me, "The thing I struggle with, that I've never found a satisfactory answer to, is if you are happy with what you have, why would you want something else? That you want to change something must mean that you're not one hundred percent content with the way things are. How can you want something else if you are okay where you are?"

I asked her to give me an example.

"So I'm a chef but because I want to be a coach, it must somehow signify that I'm dissatisfied with being a chef."

I asked her, "Really? Are they mutually exclusive? Are you unhappy being a chef?"

She said, "No. I enjoy being a chef. But I guess I *must* be unhappy though, because why else would I want something else?"

"Why *must* you be unhappy with something to want something else?" I replied. "You said that you want to get married and have kids too. Does that mean when you get married, you will need to quit coaching because you are dissatisfied with being a coach?"

She started to disqualify this by saying that being married with kids wasn't a career, but then thought about it a bit, and laughed.

"I guess being married with kids *can* be a *full-time job!*"

I was attempting to make my point that wanting something else didn't imply dissatisfaction—unless that's your experience of it! It's not a clear "if–then" statement.

I told her, "You can shave your head, move to the Himalayas, and sit under a tree, but I will tell you that your story—your inner junk—will follow you there too. That's just the way the system works. It's why we do the practice of ending dissatisfaction and suffering *here* where we are with what is going on. It's really an inside-out process."

Happiness and dissatisfaction are created. In fact, nothing *means* anything. Unless you make it mean that. Unless you indulge the notion you're dissatisfied. In which case, if that's what you believe is true, it becomes your experience. So ultimately, whatever you believe—you're *right.*

I think Henry Ford said it best in this quote attributed to him:

"Whether you think you can, or you think you can't—you're right."

The same I would say is true with my version:

"Whether you think you are happy or you think you are dissatisfied—you're right."

Now you...

Look to see what assumptions you are making about "the way things are" that may not be "the way they 'really' are."

Maybe there is no "real" way.

Be open to the possibility that there could be a belief holding this viewpoint in place.

If there is, look to see what you get by clinging to this belief.

How are you being "right" by holding on to your beliefs?

What identity is being maintained with this belief in place?

Who would you become and what would happen if this belief were no longer defining you or the situation?

_____

_____

_____

_____

_____

_____

_____

_____

ACCOUNTABILITY: THROWING RESISTANCE OUT OF THE DRIVER'S SEAT

One of the biggest issues I have seen people struggle with is keeping their commitments and staying in integrity—doing what they say they will do.

It has been a colossal struggle in my own life. It is the reason I like to design my days in such a way that I am constantly being asked to show up for others to allow me little-to-no wiggle room out of them.

For instance:

I publicly commit to projects that provide tangible evidence that I am working on them—I even started sending daily practice reminders to newsletter subscribers with a focus for the day.

I teach yoga a couple times per week, and I publicly announced that I intend to do yoga at the studio five days per week.

I also have a little experiment I am doing with a few folks on accountability that requires me to be accountable myself.

Why do I do this? Because I know that if "my life" were left in the hands of the voices, I may swerve off the path, slide down a hill and

crash into something!

I may choose a new practice that is uncomfortable, difficult, challenging, *truly beneficial for me*—get really into it—and then for some mysterious reason, quit.

It's happened before. It could happen again.

The one thing I've seen that makes a big difference for me over-and-over is accountability.

Wise words from my teacher's teacher: "You will do for the love of others what you would not be willing to do for yourself."

It is a skill that I am in fact training myself to do *for* myself and have been practicing with for sometime now:

Showing up when "I" (ego) doesn't want to.

What I am doing is moving all the things that support and nurture me onto a "non-negotiable" list.

What do I mean by this?

Consider this mundane daily ritual: Brushing your teeth.

How much energy do you put into resisting it? Not much, I imagine. You may not look forward to doing it, but really, there's not much of an internal dialog about it, right? And if there is what's the point, really? You will do it. It's part of being human and having teeth.

I bet there are other rituals in your life that you can safely say fall onto this "non-negotiable" list.

Alex Mill

But how do you do things that you know are beneficial to you but are not non-negotiable? (At least not yet—until life falls apart!) Things like meditation, eating healthy foods, exercising, working on what you love, and practicing kindness.

I'm convinced that the reason coaches, personal trainers, and buddy systems exist are to bridge this gap. They are external representations of your inner authentic, loving, compassionate being. They are kind and supportive and will take no crap from the whining, resisting, small ego that is sabotaging and ruining your life. They see through it. They understand that this is *not* you.

I know for myself that when I look at others, I can see their amazing capacity. I see infinite potential. I can also see that they may safely bury it under insecurities, doubts, and self-hatred—but that doesn't mean it isn't there.

Try it yourself. Look at someone you love who struggles with self-doubt. It's so much easier to see their talents and goodness.

Now circle around and take on the huge training opportunity to see that within yourself.

Because it *is* in all of us.

If I can see it in someone else—I know that it is there within me. I would not know it was in someone else if it was not also within me. This is the law of projection.

128

I encourage you to please sit quietly today to allow insights to drop in about this if it is not clear to you right now.

Putting this into practice:

Don't go at it alone. Find someone you can ask to keep you doing what you say you will do. Get yourself an accountability buddy.

Perhaps you keep a commitment to meditate daily for five minutes.

At the end of your day, perhaps at 8:00 pm, you check in with your buddy to say that you meditated. I would even suggest you both set recurring alarms to remind yourselves to do the check-ins. It will amaze you how good resistance is at thwarting your best-set intentions by "forgetting!"

And the check-ins don't have to be in person or even long, drawn out conversations. They can be simple text messages. A "thumb's up" emoji.

A good way to make it fun is for you to help keep your buddy accountable to some goal as well. That way it's a mutually beneficial relationship. One in which you both learn about resistance while feeling like you are giving and receiving. It will help you "see the infinite potential of the other person." It is a win-win relationship.

For this to work, it is important that you do not entertain the usual excuses, resistance, and sabotage. If one of you takes on more than is possible, do what you have committed to today and then adjust what you do the next day. If exercising for an hour like you committed to is too much—do the hour today and then commit to half-an-hour tomorrow. It really doesn't matter if you commit to something as tiny as five minutes. The important thing is that you get into a rhythm of saying you will do something and then doing it. That's it!

Here's the biggest goal in all of this: It's actually not even about doing the commitment as much as it is about seeing how resistance works. You will see what happens when you can't meditate for half-an-hour. You may say, "Okay, not a half hour, then how about fifteen minutes?" If you find that even fifteen minutes is too long, drop it to five. If five is too much and you want to quit, you can say to yourself, "Hmm... something's funny here. I can't meditate for even five minutes during my day? That seems impossible to fathom, really. Must be resistance!"

Bring it all to the light of day and see resistance for what it is—an energy-robbing vampire working against you!

It is important to do what you say you will do. You are learning to become trustworthy stewards of your life. You are learning that just because a voice in your head says "I don't feel like it" doesn't mean that you can't do it. You are proving to yourself that you do not have to feel a particular way to do something—that feelings and what you do in life—are mutually exclusive. You can transfer all of that energy being tied up in the resistance—the excuses, negotiations, whining and complaining—toward the act of doing what you said you would do. You can drop the resistance because you love yourself too much to risk letting yourself down yet again.

If a baby you love is crying in the middle of the night and you can get up when you "don't feel like it" to care for it—you can show the same compassion for yourself. Bring that love to the person inside of you who really needs it as much as that baby. This practice is teaching you that love is not "out there somewhere for me to get." It's right here inside of you.

It is the first step in throwing resistance out of the driver's seat and taking back the steering wheel of your life forever.

THE ANTI-COACH

"When someone beats a rug, the blows are not against the rug, but against the dust in it."
—Rumi

At the monastery, we had a saying that went something like this:
"If you had people in your life that treated you as badly as the voice in your head treats you, you would have gotten rid of them a long, long time ago."

Many folks have mentors, coaches, personal trainers, and loved ones who support them. Lord knows we could use one inside our own heads!

We pull through for others—we're even kind and compassionate to complete strangers like the grocery clerk—yet when it comes to ourselves, we're left with this crappy, annoying, fear-driven, constantly dissatisfied, whiny voice that berates and puts us down all day long.

Then, when it gets tired of us, it goes on to others. Have you noticed? It's an equal opportunity abuser!

So remember, if you're feeling bad, chances are good The Anti-Coach has whooshed into your life and left you a little something in your punch bowl. Time to fling it into the fan and take back your life!

WHO AM I SHOWING UP FOR?

"Receive a guest with the same attitude you have when alone. When alone, maintain the same attitude you have in receiving guests."
—*Soyen Shaku*

It was a cold Sunday morning—a blusteringly cold-cold-cold Sunday morning—when I drove out to my yoga class.

In the parking lot, I noticed my teacher's car and another minivan parked next to it. Sitting in the van was a woman who had been coming to classes the past few times. When I hopped out of the car with my gear, she also came out.

Through puffs of white breath, she wished me a good morning, and I wished her one. Then she laughed and said that if no one else showed up to class, she would have left because, "she knows what it's like to be the teacher when only one other person is there." I immediately remarked, "Oh no! Please, please, please go inside—even if you're the only one!"

Afterwards, I sat with my response to this student to see what was arising for me about it. I felt a bit of enthusiasm in my response and I wanted to look deeper. Here are a few insights:

I don't know if this is so, but I saw this student showing up (in freezing cold weather, no less) and doing this compassionate practice for herself.

Meanwhile, her rational thinking mind put her doing yoga second to "taking care" of her teacher. But was she taking care of the teacher? Let's explore this too.

Would the teacher be more thrilled to have at least one student do yoga, who braved the cold like she herself did, or to have no one show up so she could go home—*if* she would go home?

I don't know this either.

Maybe I'd heard too many stories from the monastery's early days. In the beginning, when people leading meditation groups would show up and if no one else would come, the person leading the morning meditation would sit and meditate alone. He or she would ring the bells, recite the recitations, bow and sit, then bow and leave when the meditation period was over.

To me, the question is: Why am I showing up for anything? Is it for others? Or for myself?

Or is it for something even greater? Like a commitment that I made to myself that honors integrity and places value on the act of kindness over everything else? Who am I showing up for?

YOU COUNT

In the teachings of the Buddha, there are such amazing assertions like "there is no self and other" and "everything is one."

Years ago, I saw this lesson in action at the monastery myself. Tired from a day's work, I would go home and brave my freezing cold hermitage—not having an ounce of energy to start a fire in the stove. "It's only for me and I really don't feel like it."

Only after I received the opportunity to care for a big, beautiful German Shepherd in my hermitage did I see this process of self-hatred at work.

Now that I had him to care for, it gave me permission (and the sudden willingness) to offer kindness to him by starting fires in my hermitage. And I enjoyed them too. Somehow I mustered up the energy to do this consistently.

Alone, I didn't matter. But because of him, it was okay.

This sometimes shows up when I think it would be fun to cook something new. Since I cook for myself, I hear the same rational voice say, "It's only for you—why go through all that work?"

It still takes a lot of self-mentoring to break through this and practice seeing myself as a "someone" worthy of kindness and compassion.

To say, "Yes, in fact, you matter!"

Only when you get it you matter can you live as though what you do matters. So participate. Even if you're the only one who shows up for your life.

In the end, you're all you've got.

You are counting on you.

And you count!

BEFORE YOU CAN TRUST YOURSELF, YOU MUST BECOME TRUSTWORTHY

Can you be trusted with this one precious life you have been given? Can you find that internal ally who will help you make choices coming from acceptance and compassion? Will you choose this ally instead of the anti-coach?

I talk a lot about keeping commitments as it relates to meditation. For example, I agree to sit for a particular length of time and then put it on my schedule.

It makes sense to me to set agreements like this because resistance just takes a practice such as meditation and fabricates its own "rules" about how it should go. It's always on the lookout for better deals. The next thing you know, meditation may not even resemble meditation the way they taught me how to do it. Or meditation becomes this endurance contest I must do to meet some nebulous standard.

So when I fail, what will resistance do? It will draw its conclusions for me that "this meditation stuff just doesn't work" or "it's too hard."

And I end up quitting.

So resistance/self-hate can rack up meditation as just one more thing "not for me." How handy, since one thing meditation does is to ferret out resistance and expose it for what it is and what it does!

We must keep our agreements with ourselves because what we are doing is building trust with ourselves. Before you can trust yourself, you must become trustworthy.

Imagine that you have a friend who you are counting on to show up for you and then that friend doesn't show up. You ask that friend to show up another time. And that friend continues to not show up. Repeatedly. What will happen? You will stop trusting that friend! You cannot count on that "friend!"

It's the same with you!

You are constantly being abandoned to follow the voices in your head that talk you into unhelpful activities and behaviors while ignoring the beneficial agreements you make with yourself that help you! After a time, you lose faith that anything will ever make a difference for you because you give up on yourself so easily and consistently.

Eventually, we get tricked into avoiding commitments altogether because the voices conclude, "Why bother? You will not keep them, anyway." It's very much like being hurt in love and deciding that it's best not to love anymore. We view ourselves as "lost causes" and we reduce our lives to survival. Jaded veterans of life's wars who just make do with minimal effort.

Every time you do not keep your commitments, you are becoming more and more untrustworthy with your life. This is not something to feel bad about. It's just a good thing to note and turn around!

Learning to direct your attention is a process. It's something most of us have never really been taught how to do. It's the beginning stages of becoming your own best friend. You are learning how to see yourself as a person who is perfect just as you are *and* someone worthy of all the time and attention needed to assist yourself with whatever you need to do to become whoever you want to be.

There is a deep and satisfying pleasure that comes from starting from a place of wholeness and approaching Life with the point of view that looks out and asks, "What do I want my life filled with? How would I like to spend my time? What takes care of me in the deepest and most profound way? What can I *not stand* not doing with my life? How can I support myself to become successful with this? How can I take my life out of the hands of resistance and apply kindness and compassion to it?"

Beginning with these simple steps, you will train yourself to become more and more trustworthy. You will replace what is not helpful to you with what is vital. You will swap what is mean and cruel with what is supportive and friendly. Poison with nourishment. Atrophy with fitness. Loneliness with companionship. Self-hatred with compassion.

A best friend who is trustworthy.

You!

THE CHALLENGE WITH LOVING YOURSELF

Everywhere you turn there is the same message, "You must love yourself before you can love another." Do you read that and sigh, "Yes. I *know* that. It makes perfect sense. But *how* on earth do I *do* that?"

I will admit that it sounds easier than it is. Why? Because we are up against a force that we have been trained to habitually and unconsciously follow before we can even remember. Like a two-ton magnet you see in those Bugs Bunny cartoons, our attention is yanked toward it into endless stories about what's wrong, problems, lack, deprivation, distractions, hatred, greed, pettiness, overthinking, overconfidence, fill-in-the-blank _____.

Finding compassion for yourself is acknowledging a different magnet—a draw to life, presence, and joy.

The trouble is we have been fueling the two-ton self-hate magnet with our attention for a long time. It's been in business to become powerful! It's greedy, manipulative, and downright mean. It will do anything it can to keep getting its supply of attention from you. That's what it feeds on. But if you withdraw your attention from it, it will wither, die, and you will go on your merry way—happy and scot-free!

So if you dabble in meditation and you become more committed to it, resistance will attempt to reel you back in. How? By making the issues more *real*. The more *real* the story appears to you, the more you'll scramble back to it for safety. Because it knows what you'll believe—it will use that to get you back.

Is the *real* issue your kids? If it is, you better believe it will make up stories about your kids to get you back. Is the *real* issue money? Same thing. Stories of fear and dread to tote you back in line. Soon, you'll wonder why you ever thought this meditation business was so important to you.

But our job is to sit still and see how it works. Meditation accomplishes this. How? In meditation we are practicing—like playing the violin, working out in the gym, or learning a new language. We are practicing to *consciously* direct our attention away from the stories (the two-ton magnet) and onto a very simple, portable, handy-dandy, ever present touchstone—our breath.

That's why you don't have to "clear your mind", "be a particular way", or "improve yourself." This simple act of turning the attention away from the self-hatred and to the breath is all you need to do.

The more you practice directing your attention to the breath, the better you will get at doing it all the time. And what you will find with practice is that there is a wise, compassionate presence—the intelligence of the universe that animates you—who can guide you through life perfectly.

That is who *you* are. What *you* can access. What *you* can do with this life *you* have been given.

This guide is who *you* are.

Meditation is the doorway to this guide.

I keep hammering at meditation for a reason. It's important. It's the first step inward. Everything else is merely a theory.

Alan Watts used the absurd example of walking into a restaurant and eating the menu instead of eating the meal. It's the same with reading about meditation instead of meditating. There's no benefit. I know the inspiration that comes from reading meditation books is tempting, but you have got to sit down and *do* it for anything to shift.

How to take back your life:

1. Make an agreement with yourself about how long you will sit daily. Do less than you think you should at the beginning—but at least five minutes. Everyone has five minutes. And if you don't, make a list of five-minute activities you indulge in that support feeling bad. Then stop doing those. Clear a blazing path of five-minute intervals for yourself throughout your day for meditation. It will amaze you how much time you have!

2. After making this agreement, make it visible and public. Announce it to others and to yourself. Put it on your schedule, create a poster, write it on your hand, put twist ties on your fingers, set alarms, put the meditation cushion in the middle of your room so you trip over it, tape a sign on your computer or TV set that says "Meditate *first!*"

I like to call this the "Cato and Inspector Clouseau Approach."

For those of you who have seen any of the *Pink Panther* movies, you'll recall that the inspector had an awareness buddy named Cato who hid in his house and pounced on him to keep him on his toes. This is what you are doing for yourself! (Hopefully with more gentleness.)

You will make it impossible for you to let yourself down or go to sleep on yourself (Did you smile when you read that?).

If you find that you are disarming the sirens and walking past the love notes to yourself—you may hire to work with a real Cato—a coach. Someone who refuses to be disarmed!

3. Finally, learn to talk to yourself with compassion. Practice saying out loud what you know will support you. I have a timer set up on my computer to go off every fifteen minutes and when it goes off, I stop what I'm doing, put my hands over my heart, close my eyes, turn my attention inward, and say "Thank you. I love you." Then I bow in gratitude before continuing on with my work.

When I taught yoga classes, I suggested to students that in tough poses they practice saying loving, supportive things to themselves like, "you're doing a great job" or "keep up the good work" or "I love you." Expect resistance to *hate* this idea! We haven't been trained to say this to ourselves! In fact, we have been trained to indulge the opposite.

And there will be many reasons to not even try! But could you risk it? Just as an experiment?

You can always go back to self-hate if this doesn't work.

THE UNIVERSE LOVES YOU TOO MUCH

"But life has a way of pulling the rug out from under you just when you need it least, which is what they like to call growing, I guess, but as far as I'm concerned you can have it. It seems like everything they call growing up has to jerk your guts out and just about wreck you and I've never been able to understand why that's supposed to be good for you."

—*Gary Paulsen*

"Y*ou're perfect exactly as you are.*

I love you.

I will never leave you.

I'm right here by your side—through thick and thin.

I love you unconditionally.

I care about you so much.

There's no one like you.

I'm so very proud of you.

You can share anything with me; I will always listen to you.

I see how hard you try.

It's not always easy.

I understand.

I know.

It's all going to be okay."

Sorry.

The voices in your head will never say any of these things to you. No, you won't be minding your own business someday and suddenly hear these reassuring messages playing to you in the background. It's an April Fool's gag to assume that unconditional love will be the default setting. It's never going to happen. The stream of conscious noise pollution between your ears will always dole out the opposite. The system is rigged toward feeling bad—not feeling good.

So why is that? What's the underlying message here in this? Does the universe hate our guts and life is really some cruel joke? Is our true nature hateful and mean?

The cynics would certainly have proof of that based on the premise I provided above. But what if your dilemma was really a sign that the Universe loves you too much to permit you to go unconscious? What if it wants you to be present—so you can show up to give yourself the love you deserve? What if the Universe knows that when you go unconscious, when you go up into your head and listen to the voices, you will spiral into darkness, and that this will be motivation enough to be diligently conscious, awake, and alert.

For the love of you.

You saved by you.

You embraced by you.

You holding your own hand – guiding yourself through life.

The Universe is saying, "Hey! No one, nowhere, and no thing is coming to save you. It's up to you. Will you show up for you?"

Will you?

THE SPIRIT OF INQUIRY

At the monastery where I trained, we called curiosity "the spirit of inquiry." So much of our work there was learning to notice process, or *how* things work. This was because learning *how* something worked gave us a better understanding of it. No longer was the system of suffering shrouded in mystery. We revealed it. More and more came to the surface as we dove deep.

What gets confusing in life is our obsessive focus on the *whats* of life. That partner, this job, that home, this relative. We think if we play the magic shell game with the *whats* in our lives (that car instead of this one, that girlfriend instead of this one...), switching them around until we find the right combination, we will be happy.

But in my experience that's not the way life works.

At my meditation workshops, I frequently share my favorite revelation about this process, described by this one passage:

Wanting leads to wanting. Wanting does *not* lead to having. Having leads to having. One process does not lead to another.

I saw this process in my relationship with material possessions before I went to train in the monastery. I had a nearly obsessive desire to collect books, music, videos, and stuff. I was always on the lookout for more, better, and different things. No sooner did I buy a new book, than I was hunting for another one just like it. My wanting led to more wanting. I didn't get to experience the abundance of my life by "having" it. When I started appreciating and experiencing "having" the things in my life, I started to experience satisfaction. Until then, it was a complete mystery to me why X did not equal Y. When I became curious and learned the "process" or the *how* of dissatisfaction, it became very clear to me what was going on and what I could do to make it different.

Maybe you can look to see what process you are engaged in right now—some area that's challenging for you in your life. What are you believing about it? What are you hoping to gain by being involved in it? *How* are you stuck?

Use the light of awareness to shine and illuminate these areas of darkness so you can see what is going on. And remember to set aside any judgment that arises. It is unhelpful in your journey through awareness.

AWARENESS IN ACTION

Awareness is the vast field comprising all that we can experience. In it are elements our senses can pick up on, and elements our senses can't pick up on. It's the totality of Life.

Attention moves within this field of awareness. From thing-to-thing-to-thing-to-thing—like a flashlight moving around in the darkness or a butterfly flitting from leaf to branch. One moment my attention is on the words I am typing, and in the next it quickly moves to a sound in my environment. Then it moves to how I'm feeling. Then to a thought about what I will type next, and so on.

Attention can even move and focus on the field of awareness itself!

It is important to realize how attention is directed so we can learn how to consciously direct the attention ourselves. This ability will reveal common patterns, behaviors, voices, and ultimately give us the opportunity to have the life experience we want.

The one point to keep in mind is that the voices of resistance are not going to be pleased with all of this focused attention. They will attempt to make you feel bad about all of your insights.

Expect complaints like, "You've been paying attention for so long and you still get upset by the same things!" or "This isn't working; this is too hard; you don't understand; your mind is just too out-of-control for meditation."

Please don't fall for it!

They trick so many people out of starting and fool as many into quitting. Again, remember, there is no way to do any of this wrong.

Just stick with it and pay attention. That's it. And that's everything!

WHAT IS IN THIS FOR *ME*, ANYWAY?

At the monastery, we talked about the distinction of "bringing spiritual practice into my life," versus "bringing my life into spiritual practice."

If I am *using* spiritual practice—mindfulness, meditation, chanting, visualizations, breathing techniques, etc. to better *my* life—subtly, it's an acknowledgement that I must somehow "improve myself," "fix myself," "change for my own good," "cope with the world"—whatever. It's like the ego is saying, "Frankly, what's in this for *me?*"

Because we are so results driven, it just makes sense to approach even spiritual practices this way. I mean, why do something if we don't get the good stuff from it? Right?

However, from my perspective, there's a different attitude of mind I access when I hear "I bring my life into spiritual practice."

For me, it's one of humility, surrender, and trust. It's like I'm saying that *Life* knows best and I am not doing this—I am allowing myself to get out of my way so that Life can live through me.

The caterpillar doesn't go out someday and say, "I will make this transformation business happen for me by becoming a better being. I will be a butterfly, gosh darnit!" On the contrary, that caterpillar has Life on its side to deal with the *how* of it. That caterpillar just needs to keep showing up and keep doing what it does to facilitate this process. For the caterpillar, transformation is *inevitable* because of its practice.

Today, look to see how you can be like that caterpillar. Surrender to your practice.

And if you don't have one, and would like one, see if you can start from the understanding that

Your practice is a gift to life.

Begin by accepting yourself. This is the starting point.

As a *whole, complete* person. Then allow your light to shine forth!

So let the transformation happen *to* you as you continue to *show up* and *let go* of what is in your way.

This is a very different approach than *making* transformation happen by *getting* more and more for yourself.

THE HOLE PROBLEM

Imagine a world that had a unique problem:

Everyone was falling into a hole.

Over-and-over, people kept falling into this hole.

It was a misery.

No one had a good solution.

One guy beat himself up for falling into the hole. He assumed that the beating would prevent him from doing it again. That it would teach him. But it didn't. He kept falling in. He kept getting a beating. And he learned nothing.

Another gal decided to pad herself up so that when she fell into the hole — it wouldn't hurt as much. But it still did. It was a pretty big drop. She sighed because it was the best she could come up with. So she kept stuffing herself to keep the pain away.

Another decided never to walk again. He figured that if he didn't walk, there was no way to fall into the hole. But in the long run, this didn't work. He needed to get up eventually. And it was only a matter of time before he fell into the hole like the rest of society did. When he got out, he vowed *never* to walk around again.

Another decided to toughen her character. So when she fell into the hole, she would pretend like it wasn't a big deal. She got to be "Super Gal." And she silently suffered alone. Despite her powerful tumbling act, she was broken and bruised like everyone else.

The methods of compensations, alterations, tactics, strategies, and antics were all the rage in the media.

Experts labeled the problem "holeaphobia", "droppression", and "ADHD (Awful Dropping in Hole Disorder.)"

There were even pills of all sorts created to erase the hole from people's thoughts (should they be able to afford the high price to have them prescribed!) Dropping into the hole, for these people, was replaced with numbness.

Once upon a time, a very patient gal had this radical idea to sit very still. She began paying attention. She started to look inward. She noticed that as she simply sat, she became aware of some really interesting things.

This didn't stop her from falling into the hole. But she persisted with her reflections.

One day, while she sat still, she made a startling discovery. She became aware that her eyes were closed! They suddenly flicked open for the first time!

With eyes wide open, she remarked, "My goodness! I've been falling into this hole because I couldn't see it!"

And sure enough, she looked around at the world and saw everyone with their eyes closed!

"How simple!" she remarked.

She did a little experiment. She walked up to the edge of the hole, stopped before it, and did not fall in.

The hole was no longer a mystery to her.

She didn't need to change. She didn't need to improve herself, (there was nothing wrong with her.) She didn't need a beating. She didn't need protection. She didn't need pills. She didn't need anything to be different.

She was overjoyed!

But, unsatisfied to be the only one with this amazing awareness, she began sharing her discovery with the world.

At first the people thought she was crazy.

Eyes squeezed shut, with heads shaking, they complained, "That's way too simple."

But eventually some of them, tired of dropping, decided to sit in patience like she did so they too could see. Something was obviously working for her.

Some kept at it, and learned how to open their eyes like she did. Others gave up and resorted to the latest fads of the day.

Over time, many stopped falling into the hole. And some who had tried but gave up, made a commitment to try again.

They were diligent in their practice.

They saw that opening their eyes revealed the hole problem.

Perhaps they would inspire others to do the same.

Meditation and Reinventing Yourself Bonus Stuff!

What?!

I'm excited to announce that I've got a special page on my website with *Bonus Stuff* just for you!

Want to tack the full-color *Meditation Poster* on page 7 up to your wall without cutting it out of this book?

How about the *Choose Your Own Adventure* mini-booklet on page 149? Would you like to see it as an animated flipbook? Or print, cut, fold, and assemble a copy for yourself?

Loved the *art* and need it adorning your walls (or a shirt)?

Perhaps you're ready to dive in and do an online *Zen meditation workshop* with me!

Well, hang on to your seat girls and boys, because you can get all of this awesome sauce (and more!) on my website here...

bonus.meditationandreinventingyourself.com

ACKNOWLEDGEMENTS

First, I would like to thank my beautiful, brilliant and compassionate life partner, Karen Davis, for her endless love and support. She has been my beacon of light and my champion. We spent hours (and hours) together assembling and editing the first edition of this book so that it would be ready for our live event with Steve Chandler back in 2015. This book would not be what it is had it not been for her.

Thank you to Steve Chandler. What can I say? You have gone out of your way to help me. You've promoted me, given me opportunities to share my work with your community, coached me, shared your wisdom on stage with me, and modeled for me what being a good man is. I have so much to learn from you. Deep, deep respect, love and light to you.

Thank you to all my clients and students. You took the plunge! You decided to invest in yourself and in your transformation. You hired me as your coach and you've done the work in my online retreat(s). Your support of the practice makes it possible for me to write books like this and keep sharing the teachings to everyone who crosses my path. My interactions with you have kept the practice alive within my heart. You require both of us to show up when the voices say, "You don't want to."

Deep Gasshō to my teacher, the Buddhas, the monks, the Zen monastery, the Sangha, and all those who came before us to make this wonderful practice available. The world so desperately needs practice and all of us stewards to keep it alive and well.

Thank you to Mom, Dad, and Andy for being my family. I appreciate you for always being there for me no matter how unusual my life decisions can appear to be.

And last but not least, thanks to Jax, the furry, four-legged Zen Master who so diligently trains me every day.

ABOUT THE AUTHOR

Alex Mill is a Zen Life Coach. He trained in a Zen monastery for nearly 14 years and now offers his extensive experience to help people transform their lives and businesses from the inside-out through mindfulness, meditation, and compassionate self-mentoring practices.

He is the creator of two life-changing, 30-day online retreats, *Heart-to-Heart: Compassionate Self-Mentoring,* and its sequel, *Help Yourself to Change* (both filled with cartoons like the ones in this book).

He offers an online version of his Zen meditation workshop entitled, *Taming Your Inner Noise,* where you can learn how to meditate and experience why meditation is so important.

He is the author of several other books on Zen awareness practice including *Practicing Presence, The Zen Life: Spiritual Training for Modern Times, A Shift to Love: Zen Stories and Lessons by Alex Mill,* and three mini guidebooks, *Living the Zen Life: Practicing Conscious, Compassionate Awareness.*

If you'd like to learn more about Zen Life Coaching, please go to his website, coaching@zenlife.coach, and send an email requesting more information.

Alex lives in Louisville, Colorado with his partner in compassionate transformation, Karen Davis, and their English Crème Retriever, the aggressive cuddler, Prince Jax, Master of All He Surveys (Jax for short).

You can read more about Alex's books, retreats, workshops and latest offerings at www.zenlife.coach.

BOOKS BY ALEX MILL

Practicing Presence

The Zen Life: Spiritual Training
for Modern Times

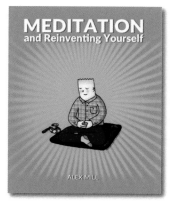

Meditation and Reinventing Yourself

A Shift to Love: Zen Stories and
Lessons by Alex Mill

Living the Zen Life: Practicing Conscious, Compassionate Awareness

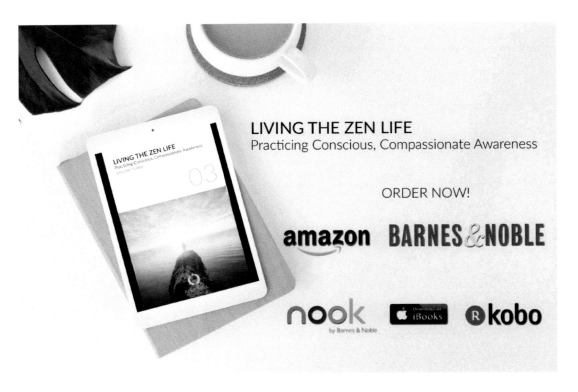

PROGRAMS BY ALEX MILL

Taming Your Inner Noise: A Zen
Meditation Workshop

Heart-to-Heart: Compassionate
Self-Mentoring

Help Yourself to Change

Made in the USA
Monee, IL
28 January 2020